Biographies of Great African People

DUSE MUHAMMAD ALI

Faheem Judah-EL D.D.

BISMILLAH AR-RAHMAN AR-RAHEEM

Begin All things with the Illustrious Name of Allah, The Most Gracious, Most Merciful

Dusé Mohamed Ali (Bey Effendi), (21 November 1866 - 25 June 1945) (دوسي محمد علي), was an African nationalist. Note* ***Bey*** *(Moorish: Used by the Moors بك Beg, Beğ) is a title for* ***chieftain/ Moorish Chief,*** *traditionally applied to the leaders of small tribal groups.* ***(See Almohades and Almoravides)***

The word "Bey" means "Rabb" (Arabic) or Lord. Beys ruled provinces which were called "beyliks".

Ali was also an actor, historian, journalist, editor, lecturer, traveller, publisher, and founder of the Comet Press Ltd, and The Comet newspaper in Nigeria.

Duse Ali's Early life

He was born in Alexandria, Egypt (Kemet). His father, Abdul Salim Ali, was an Officer in the Egyptian Army and died in active service at the battle of Tel-el-Kiber Egypt, in the year 1882. His mother was Sudanese. Ali would eventually lose his knowledge of Arabic and contact with his family in Egypt.

Battle of Tel-El-Kebir An Anglo-Army against the Egyptian Army.

General Sir Garnet Wolseley against Ahmed Arabi Bey .

The Egyptian army was probably around 20,000 strong with 60 guns. The British and Indian force comprised 11,000 infantry, 2,000 cavalry and 45 guns. Duse Ali's father died in the battle.

British cavalry capturing Egyptian soldiers after the Battle of Tel El Kebir. Illustration by R Caton Woodville for the Illustrated London News.

Duse Ali goes to Study abroad

Duse received his early training in Egypt (Kemet), but at the age of 9 was sent to England to be educated, until the death of his father forced him to return back to Egypt (Kemet). After mourning the death of his father he returned to England again, still a minor child and under the care of Canon Berry, Duse pursued his studies at King's College London where his was an excellent student.

Duse's father always wanted him to become a Doctor, following the school of Tehuti, and Duse actually started medical school when he heard the news of his father's death. Left to make his own choice, Duse decided to become an actor and later on a journalist. Always having the urge to express himself and go on stage, he left his medical studies. On completing his studies at the University of London and perfecting his craft, he went on stage in London where he distinguished himself as a great Thespian, and as time went on Duse Muhammad Ali was ranked alongside the world's greatest actors of his time.

NOT A SELL OUT

Duse Ali love Africa, and African people, he was a strong African nationalist with strong Pan-Africanist views. He was a devout Muslim, and performed Dawah in every city he visited.

Note The word "Da'wah" in Arabic simply means to invite to something. When it is used in conjunction with Islam it is understood to mean "Inviting to the Way of submission and surrender to Allah."*

"Kuntum khairan ummatin ukhrajat linaasi tawmaruna bil maruf wa tan anna anhil munkar."
You are the best of people raised up, for you call to all that is right and righteous and you forbid the evil, and you believe in Allah.
[Qur'an 3:110]

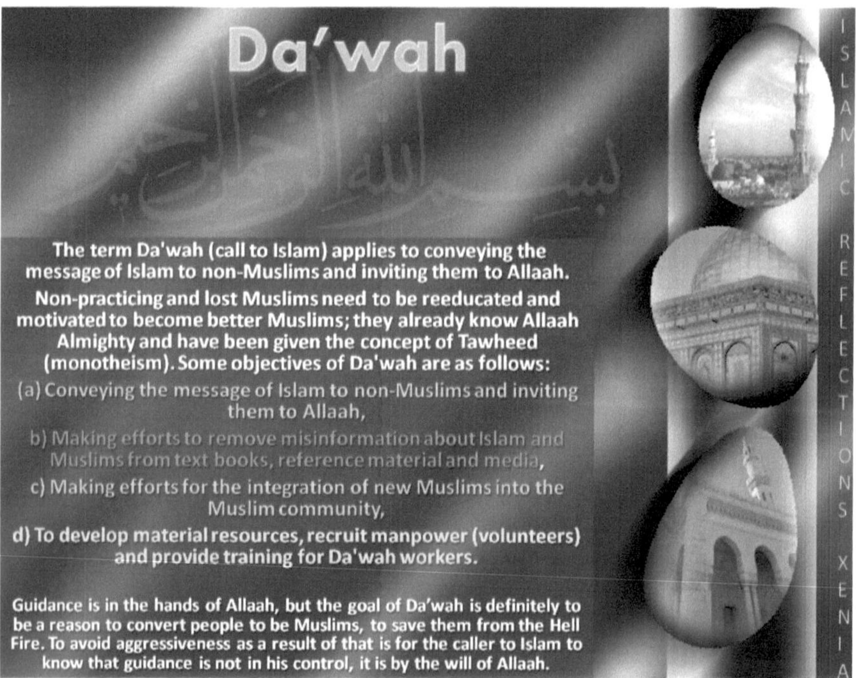

In 1926 Duse Ali established the Universal Islamic Society in Detroit Michigan which was the model for both Noble Drew Ali's Moorish Science Temple and Wallace Fard Muhammad's Nation of Islam. The Universal Islamic Society was one of the main sources for information and lessons for both organizations. This Islamic-Pan-African influence can be seen in Marcus Garvey's motto "One God, One Aim, One Destiny.

NOBLE DREW ALI

NOBLE DREW ALI

Wallace Fard Muhammad – W.F. Fard

THE MOST HONORABLE MARCUS M. GARVEY

The lasting effects of Duse Ali's social and academic efforts are long lasting, and far-reaching. These influences were not seen directly in the great Marcus Garvey, but in those to whom Garvey mentored, such as Noble Drew Ali and The Honorable Elijah Muhammad who was an early supporter of the Universal Negro Improvement Association and African Communities League's (UNIA) Detroit chapter before joining the Nation of Islam and becoming Elijah Muhammad). Both of Malcolm X's parents were also members of UNIA. Duse Ali's beliefs and Pan African view can be found among these movements and their leaders, such as Black Pride, the idea of a land base, Africa Culture, African knowledge of self, and return to African primordial religion/spirituality.

THE HONORABLE ELIJAH MUHAMMAD WEARING THE TARBOOSH

THE HONORABLE ELIJAH MUHAMMAD

THE HONORABLE MALCOLM X

EL HAJJ MALIK SHABAZZ

Malcolm making salaat

Actor and playwright

Duse Ali was also in the company of Herbert Beerbohm Tree and in Mrs. Langtry's Antony and Cleopatra production, at the Royal Princess Theatre, London. Ali also toured England, Ireland and Scotland. He produced Othello and The Merchant of Venice at Hull, Yorkshire, in 1902, playing the parts of Othello and the Prince of Morocco, and winning the plaudits of the British Press.

Herbert Beerbohm Tree

Antony and Cleopatra

Othello The Moor

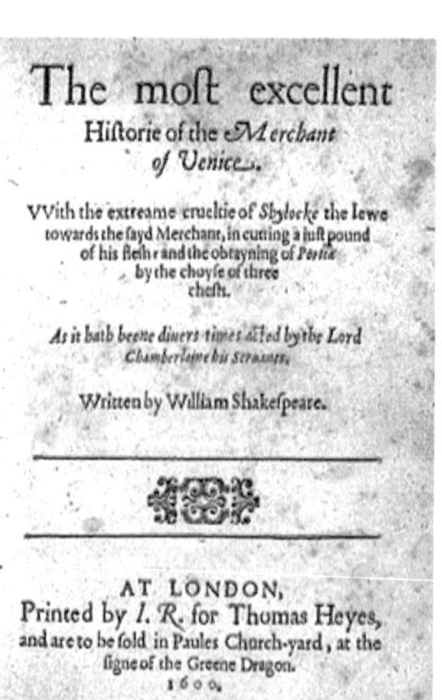

The moſt excellent
Hiſtorie of the *Merchant of Venice.*

VVith the extreame crueltie of *Shylocke* the Iewe towards the ſayd Merchant, in cutting a iuſt pound of his fleſh: and the obtayning of *Portia* by the choyſe of three cheſts.

As it hath beene diuers times acted by the Lord Chamberlaine his Seruants.

Written by William Shakeſpeare.

AT LONDON,
Printed by *I. R.* for Thomas Heyes,
and are to be ſold in Paules Church-yard, at the ſigne of the Greene Dragon.
1600.

The Merchant of Venice

Duse Ali was a very talented playwright, Among his credits he produced **The Jew's Revenge** at the Royal Surrey Theatre in London in 1903, **A Cleopatra Night** at Dundee in 1907, and the **Lily of Bermuda**, a musical comedy produced at the Theatre Royal, Manchester, in 1909.

The British and American press welcomed Ali's productions with welcomed arms and rave reviews. His greatest production and performance was in "**A Daughter of Judah"**, which was first produced in the Glasgow Empire Theatre, in 1906.

A Daughter of Zion

The London Daily Telegraph Reviewed "A Daughter of Zion and wrote: "Duse Mohamed is an actor of outstanding merit."

He also wrote and produced a variety of plays in America, and as an actor his talent was praised by American audiences as well as critics. Ali also found fame in the field of sociology where he was honored in England as notable Sociologist.

Note* Duse Ali used his Sufi Knowledge to heal and solve problems for many people.

He founded the Hull Shakespeare Society, of which Sir Henry Irving was the first President; the Anglo-Ottoman Society, London, which included Lords Newton, Lamington, Stourton and Mowbray.

Sir Henry Irving

In 1915 Ali founded and was Secretary of the Indian Muslim Soldiers' Widows' and Orphans' War Fund, and among the patrons were Consuelo the Duchess of Marlborough, the Honorable D. Lloyd George, Sir Edward Grey, Lord and Lady Lamington, Lord and Lady Newton, the Marquis and Marchioness of Crew, Mrs. H. H. Asquith, Sir Austen and Lady Chamberlain, Lord Curzon, and almost all the members, of the British Cabinet.

Consuelo, the Duchess of Marlborough

Patron of Duse Ali's Indian Muslim Soldiers' Widows' and Orphans' War Fund

Sir Edward Grey

Patron of Duse Ali's Indian Muslim Soldiers' Widows' and Orphans' War Fund

The Right Hon. D. Lloyd George

Patron of Duse Ali's Indian Muslim Soldiers' Widows' and Orphans' War Fund

Mrs. H. H. Asquith

Patron of Duse Ali's Indian Muslim Soldiers' Widows' and Orphans' War Fund

Lecturer and Journalist

In 1925 Ali founded the Universal Islamic Society and the America-Asia Association where he was president. He published a newspaper called **"The Land of the Pharaohs"** (published in London and New York in 1911). "The Land of the Pharaohs" newspaper was a history of Egypt (Kemet) that "became a significant contribution to the decolonization of the minds of African people in the Caribbean, the United States and West Africa".

In 1911 the first Universal Races Congress was held at the University of London. After the Congress, Ali founded the African Times and Orient Review in London, with the help of John Eldred Jones, a journalist from Sierra Leone.

DUSE GETS FINANCIAL SUPPORT

Duse Ali preached unity among African people, cooperation, and self-determination, and these words found the ears of a group of West African leaders visiting London. The West African Group gave Ali the financial assistance he needed to launch the paper. The West African group included J. E. Casely Hayford, Francis T. Dove and C. W. Betts from Sierra Leone and Dr. Oguntola Sapara from Lagos.

The Honorable J. E. Casely Hayford

Dr. Oguntola Sapara from Lagos Nigeria

As a political, cultural, and Pan African journal advocating Pan African Unity and Asian nationalism Ali created a forum for African intellectuals and activists from around the world. His struggle for equality and self-determination for African and Asian people through his many forums drew the attention of a wide variety of contributors. Among the contributors were great writers such as **George Bernard Shaw, H. G. Wells, Lord Lytton, Annie Besant, Sir Harry H. Johnston, Henry Francis Downing, William H. Ferris and Marcus Garvey,** who frequently visited his beloved mentor at his Fleet Street office.

The journal covered issues dealing with the plight of African and Asian people in the United States, the Caribbean, West Africa, South Africa, and Egypt, as well as in Asia, including India, China, and Japan. Garvey, who was living in London at the time, worked for Ali and contributed an article to the journal's October 1913 issue. It ceased publication in October 1918, and was succeeded by the African and Orient Review, which operated through most of 1920.

George Bernard Shaw

H.G. Wells

Lord Lytton

Annie Besant

Sir Harry H. Johnston

Henry Francis Downing

William Henry Ferris (1874-1941)

Marcus Garvey

Ali was a contributor to several leading European and American periodicals and his articles were translated and published in Germany, France, Austria, Turkey, Egypt, Japan and West Africa. In the year following the last issue of the African and Orient Review, Ali traveled to the United States, never returning to Britain again. There he worked in Garvey's **Universal Negro Improvement Association movement**, contributing articles on African issues to the African World, and heading a department on African affairs.

He wrote and published The Hull Coronation Ode, a history of Hull in verse, in 1902, a copy of which was presented to **His Majesty King Edward VII.**

In Europe Duse Ali was recognized as an authority on Oriental affairs, political and social issues.

Duse Ali Travels to Nigeria

Duse Ali's first visit to Nigeria was in July 1921. He arrived to a historic reception by the entire Lagos community held at the Islamic Mosque. He went back to Lagos again in 1931 on businesses, which lead to his appointment as editor of the Nigerian Daily Times Newspaper.

On Monday, October 3rd 1932, Ali produced the play **"A Daughter of Pharaoh**" which played in the Glover Memorial Hall, Lagos Nigeria. Daughter of Pharaoh was a smash hit, and according to the review from the Daily Times: **"Daughter of Pharaoh set a new standard in Lagos entertainment".**

Before long Ali assumed the editorial seat of the Nigerian Daily Telegraph, bring aboard Ayo Lijadu as his immediate assistant. Ali began publication of The Comet as a weekly newspaper on

27 July 1933. He nurtured and inspired the Muslim community in Nigeria, preaching to them about the upliftment of African people, and the upliftment of humanity. It would be Marcus Garvey who would make Ali's famous quote: **"One God, One Aim, One Destiny"** a household phrase amongst conscious African people worldwide.

Duse Mohamed Ali makes his transformation

Following an illness, Mohamed Ali made his transformation from this world at the age of 78 in the Nigerian Hospital, Lagos Nigeria, on 25 June 1945. His funeral took place on the afternoon of Wednesday, 27 June 1945. It was attended by a large group of admirers of Ali, and the Muslim community. The mourners numbered well over 5,000 consisting of people from various walks of life including political, social and religious leaders.

A Khutba (sermon) in English was delivered by Mr. L. B. Agusto, President of the Islamic Society of Nigeria, who paid glowing tributes to the life of Duse Mohamed Ali, A short oration in Arabic was also delivered by Mr. D. Couri, a friend of the Ali's.

Led by the **Ansaarullah Community, and the Ansaar Ud Deen school children**. Muslim women, the executives of all Muslim Societies taking the rear, the funeral procession went through Victoria streets and other prominent through fares watched by a crowd who lined the Streets to Okesuna Muslim

Cemetery where Duse Mohamed Ali, the devout Muslim, Pan-Africanist, veteran journalist, author and actor was committed to mother earth.

Wreaths were laid by Madam Gertrude La Page (wife), Mr. and Mrs. A. S. W. Shackle ford, Mr. and Mrs. V. Renwick, Mr. and Mrs. M. A. Ogun and staff of the Nigerian Bureau of Publicity, Miss Moss, **The Rosicrucian Fellowship Lagos Group Centre,** Young Muslim Society, Federation of Master Printers, Mrs. Otunba Payne, Moslem Reading Circle, and staff of the Comet Press Ltd., Mr. and Mrs. S. H. Pearce and Miss Remi Pearce and many others.

Among those present were Herbert Macaulay, Karimu Kotun, J. T. White, Dr. I. Nimbe, Messrs. S. L. Akitola, and Olatunji Idewu (Daily Service), I. B. Thomas, (Akede Eko), Tony Enahoro, (Daily Comet), Delu Akitoye, C. N. Jellicoe Johnson, S.M. Kadiku, M. S. Jibril Martin, Messrs. F. I. George, M. A. Ogun, Ferdinand Stine Morocco-Clarke, John Adcbayo, Revs. J. A. Idowu, and D. A. Bababunmi.

CITED WORKS

References

1. David Dabydeen, John Gilmore, Cecily Jones, The Oxford Companion to Black British History, Oxford University Press, 2007, p. 25.
2. Imanuel Geiss (1974). The Pan-African Movement: a history of pan-Africanism in America, Europe, and Africa. Taylor & Francis. p. 223 ISBN 0-8419-0161-9.
3. Faheem Judah-EL D.D., Biographies of Great African People, Axum Press, 2013.
4. A Daughter of the Congo - Simple English, the free encyclopedia
5. Ferris, William Henry (1874-1941) | The Black Past: Remembered and Reclaimed
6. L. B. Augusto - Google Search
7. Faheem Judah-EL D.D., Biographies of Great African People Vol. 2, Axum Press, 2013.

AXUM PUBLICATIONS

THE ORDER OF
MELCHIZEDEK MAGAZINE
YOUR SOURCE TO THE PATH
OF ENLIGHTENMENT
FAHEEM JUDAH-EL

HOW TO MARRY
A COUPLE OF THE
ABYSSINIAN
TABERNACLE OF
THE MOST HIGH
FAHEEM JUDAH-EL

THE REAL
MEANING OF SUFI
REVISED EDITION
FAHEEM JUDAH-EL

THE SCIENCE OF THE 99 BEAUTIFUL NAMES OF THE MOST HIGH GOD

FAHEEM JUDAH-EL

MALCOLM X
PROPHET OF OUR
TIME RELEVANT
SPEECHES OF
TODAY

SPIRITUAL ARCHAEOLOGY THE FIRST DEGREE

FAHEEM JUDAH-EL

KHAMITIAN MYSTICS
MAGAZINE
"SEEKERS OF THE WAY"
AXUM PUBLICATIONS
www.lulu.com/egipt

WHO ARE THE SONS
OF GOD?
FAHEEM JUDAH-EL

WHO KNOWS THE SECRETS?
SPIRITUAL
SERIES
ONE
FAHEEM JUDAH-EL

Biographies of Great African People

DUSE MUHAMMAD ALI

ISBN 978-1-300-88590-0

www.ingramcontent.com/pod-product-compliance
Ingram Content Group UK Ltd.
Pitfield, Milton Keynes, MK11 3LW, UK
UKHW041835200726
13854UKWH00003BA/1146